THE RECRUITMENT OFFICER

BY

THOMAS ALEXANDER

The Recruitment Officer by Thomas Alexander

Direct Light Publications
45 Dudley Court, Endell Street, London, WC2H 9RF

Permissions may be sought directly from Publishing Rights Department 45 Dudley Court, Endell Street, London, WC2H 9RF
performance@directlight-publications.com

Library of Congress Cataloguing in Publication Data
Application submitted.
British Library Cataloguing in Publication Data
Application submitted.
03 04 05 06 07 08 10 9 8 7 6 5 4 3
ISBN 978-1-941979-13-6

–

Edited by Shirin Laghai for Direct Light Publications.

Cover Design by SimplyA

The Recruitment Officer

SYNOPSIS

Tom, a charming Yankee recruiter comes to an unspecified English town and falls in love with the conference centre manager, Julia.

But what exactly is he recruiting for? Why does everyone who joins never return, and what's on the other side of the door he ushers them through?

When Julia starts to get interested in joining Tom tries to do everything to dissuade her, but who is he protecting and what exactly are the benefits of becoming a recruit?

An existential love story that asks questions of who we are, what we want from life and whether we're getting it, The Recruitment Officer is a remodelling of the 1706 play by George Farquhar, *The Recruiting Officer.*

ABOUT THE AUTHOR

Thomas Alexander has worked in almost all forms of theatre, from opera to children's performances, working as everything from stage hand to costume designer, and has seen his work translated into four different languages and performed as far afield as America and Afghanistan.

His plays, along with his first novel, *A Scattering Of Orphans*, have been published by Direct Light Publications.

Also by the Author

PLAYS

Happiness
Murder Me Gently
The Family
Begat
The Crossroads Country
Great
The Visitor
When Dusk Brings Glory
The Recruitment Officer
Writer's Block
The Last Christmas
Writing William
The Big Match

ONE ACT PLAYS

Four Widows and A Funeral
For Arts Sake
The TV
Life TM
The Dance
The Pink Cow

ADAPTATIONS

William Shakespeare's R3
Othello

NOVELS

A Scattering Of Orphans

FOREWORD

In the summer of 2013 a small collection of my plays were being performed under the banner of A Space Between Words, a novel idea that saw staged readings of produced and unproduced plays alike stage-read in front of a live audience and streamed over the internet.

I was, at the time, teaching politics and psychology at a boarding school in central London, which was where I saw a production of George Farquhar's The Recruiting Officer at the wonderful Donmar Warehouse, which was just around the corner from my apartment.

Although it was brilliantly produced, I can't say it was my favourite play, not even of the season, and I'm ashamed to say that my mind started to wander, starting to wonder about the more existential ideals that were being brought out from the text.

In Farquhar's The Recruiting Officer, the quest for love and the quest for soldiers to fight in a war are juxtaposed, so that through the standard girl-dressed-like-a-boy-who-confuses-everyone contrivance Farquhar can contrast the morality of seeking a wife with the morality of signing up soldiers to their doom.

I had, for my part, wanted to write a love story for adults for quite a while. A middle-aged attraction built on compatibility rather than lust, but I also wanted to explore some of the difficulties of 'reawakening'. Love reigniting the passions of youth in a couple, a love affair rekindling a love for life, a love for exploration, and, more importantly, what would happen if those two were in direct opposition.

By the time the house came down on the Donmar's production of The Recruiting Officer, I had the nucleus of my 'Recruit-ment' Officer pretty much set.

I wrote The Recruitment Officer then with the direct idea of it being part of The Space Between Words. I wanted it, naturally, to be stageworthy but I also wanted to it to be a strong talking-heads piece, something that wouldn't require the overt staging of some of my other plays.

Everyone loves a good monologue and I'm no different in that regard, but 21st century theatre is not easily given to such indulgence. The spoken word and its rhythms – when it comes to theatre at least – has returned to the banter of Shakespearian comedies and that, on the whole, is a good thing. But there's something about a monologue, not just for an actor but for the audience as well, that resonates. Like a film director, lingering on a shot, the lens soaking up the character's depths and conceits, slowly but unrelentingly closing in on its subject, drawing you in, a good monologue should make you forget you are looking at an actor and leave nothing but you and the character in front of you.

The live-reading of The Recruitment Officer was held in an old abandoned BBC radio station on Marylebone High St. In one of those wonderful arts movements that rarely happens anywhere else, the government had leased the building to an arts community while they wondered whether to try and sell it or pull it down completely.

The building housed artists, entrepreneurs, rehearsals, and, for one weekend, us. We found an old recording studio on the second floor, where the wires had been stripped and the walls covered from floor to ceiling with pages from old books. Yellowing pages plastering over clipped plaster and exposed windows giving it an eerily transcendental light that we thought fitted the piece perfectly.

We worked with some amazing talent, all of whom are listed on one of the pages here, and though I don't think I realized how sad the play had become – almost an homage to the futility of life – I thoroughly enjoyed the production, the strange settings and the immediacy of the effect it had.

Of all the plays I have written and seen produced, The Recruitment Officer is then by far the most 'London' of them: conceived in the Donmar, written on a balcony in Covent Garden for production in Marylebone with a view to a London audience. I don't think anything else I have written to be more Capital bound than that, despite the fact that it is neither set, nor houses any characters from that city at all.

Who knows? Perhaps that's where the 'door' leads.

Thomas Alexander – 2014

Cast of Characters

No of cast: 5/7

TOM - Middle Aged. Southern American.
JULIA - Middle Aged. English.
DAVE - Middle Aged. English.
MALE 1
FEMALE 1
MALE 2
FEMALE 2

The Recruitment Officer was originally performed in London in 2013.

Produced by The Space Between Words it was directed by Alec Harris.

TOM - Robert Blackwood

JULIA - Katie Richmond

DAVE - Andrew Lambert-Knott

MALE 1 - Adam Carpenter

FEMALE 1 - Pauline Menear

MALE 2 - Sophia Wrightman

FEMALE 2 - Shirin Laghai

The Recruitment Officer

ACT 1

ACT 1

SCENE 1

A HALL.

TOM IS STANDING IN FRONT OF AN AUDIENCE, OUR AUDIENCE, ADDRESSING THEM AS IF AT A CONVENTION. BEHIND HIM A DOOR, NONDESCRIPT EXCEPT FOR THE FACT THAT IT ISN'T ATTACHED TO ANY SORT OF WALL, STANDS.

THE DOOR IS CLOSED.

TOM   We're running a bit behind, so if we can get started… (PAUSE) Before we do; you all have your sheets? Yeah? Like this one? Have a look under your seat if you… excellent. Okay, right. (CHANGE) I do not believe in acceptance. Maybe you do, maybe you don't, but I'm standing here, today, to tell you that such a thing does not exist!

And yet we do it. Every day. In a million different ways. We accept that the ground is not going to fly away from our feet! We accept that the sun is gonna shine or the wind is going to blow or the person we love is going to be nice to us about our weight. (PAUSE) That's not what I'm talking about.

I'm talking about acceptance of reality. Acceptance of who we are, of what we are told we can be. Acceptance, ladies and gentlemen; and I for one, do not believe in it!

When we are children, back in that time that many of us

cannot remember, before the dinosaurs for some of us. Back in that time, we had the perfect tool against acceptance, the perfect broom with which to sweep it away! Wonder! Wonder, ladies and gentlemen was the very thing that stood between us and acceptance and wonder is what I want to talk to you about tonight!

When I was a child... When I was young, we didn't live in a big house. We didn't have the kind of garden children could run around in or... play ball or anything like that. My parents they were, well, they were hard working, that's what they were. Hard working. Honest. And so we grew up in a house that did not have many opportunities for wonder.

I always wanted to... you know what I'm talking about... I always wanted to grow up in one of those houses that had bookcase doors and secret passages. You know what I mean? I tell you, each and every library I set foot in I used to yank at a book hoping it was a trigger.

Ahh, because, we read about that, don't we!? We read about secret corridors that lead to secret towers and mazes that run from the end of your gate. Reality; well that might not be the most interesting of places, but we never lose that sense of wonder! No, we do not. We never stop hoping!

A DOOR OPENS BEHIND HIM, LIGHT STREAMING FROM IT ONTO THE STAGE.

Every door; every door holds a possibility for us. Wherever we are; no matter how bad it is, no matter how good, every door is the possibility of something better. A better world! A better life, out there waiting for us. Full of... well, that's the thing, isn't it! That's the very point! We have no idea!

You cannot explain wonder. To a child; you cannot explain why the sun comes up, why the moon goes down. These things have no place in a child's mind. As questions? Sure! But the answers? The answers?! They are as real to us as children as… dragons and unicorns!

What lies behind that door… is another door, and another and another and that's what wonder is! The idea that out there, out beyond the horizons of our six year old heads; is something that cannot be explained!

PAUSE.

And then we grow up!

My father… I didn't see a lot of my father. Hard work means being away a lot and, well, we can all attest to that, but my father, he was a door maker. A door maker. Not a locksmith, he made doors.

You wouldn't think that would take him away that much, but… gone he was. All hours of the day. They'd need a new building and they'd say to themselves. Building's probably going to need doors!

So out he'd go, day and night. Talking doors like they were the second coming. Big doors, small doors. House was littered with them. Now, like I said, this wasn't a house that was full of wonder! This wasn't a house of libraries and towers. No. But it was a house full of doors! Every wall was covered with them! Big doors, small doors, left-handed doors, door that opened up and doors that fell down 'cos, well, they weren't attached to anything really! See, these weren't doors that led to places. These weren't doors that had other rooms on the other side. No, these were his samples; leaned up against any old thing. Not a square foot of our house wasn't taken up with a door of some kind. Eight, nine doors a room, propped up against any old thing! Sometimes, we'd forget which ones actually led somewhere! Man could be trapped in a room like that for days.

But that didn't matter. No. Not to us children. That didn't matter at all.

Wonder!

I weren't expecting no grey wall when I opened them up. I was expecting… jungles, sky castles, sunsets! And it didn't matter how many times I opened them up, neither. Disappointment wasn't part of it! 'Cos I knew, I knew as sure as I knew a mother's love that if I opened them; the right one, at just the right time… wonder!

Nothing but concrete on the other side last time? Wouldn't be this time! I just kept opening those doors expecting something to pop out. Didn't matter if it was dust. Which, I can assure you, drove my mother up the wall. Didn't matter if it was. Opening doors is the only thing they're built for.

'Cos I knew, I just knew; one day I was going to open one of those doors and whoosh! I'd be gone.

I don't need to ask you when the last time was you felt like that.

I don't need to ask you the last time you felt anything even close to it.

My father, he used to have this saying; life, he'd say. Life is the great leveller. And that's what we are. Make no mistake about it! Level! We get to a point in our lives where basically that's all we are with it! Just picking up the days; count…

count… One day after another! One foot in front of the other. No point in where we're going. No point in looking where we've been. Same old landscape! Same footstep after the other!

They got that story. The footprints on the beach? Two, one, two, one. Always made me wonder… why aren't none of you swimming!

Because life, ladies and gentlemen, life is something we choose. It does not come to us. It does not seek us out. We got to look for it. And, ladies and gentlemen, if you are sitting here, right now; sought it out you have!

We all walk through doors. You all walked through one to get here tonight. You'll all walk through one to get out again. Only thing you got to ask yourself is; is it gonna be the same one, the one you walked in through? Or is it gonna be a new one? A special one, the last one, the very epitome of a once in a lifetime's offer!

Everybody… At some point everybody has thought about walking through this door. There's a reason more people use us than any other supplier. Everyone has thought about walking through that door!

For some, it's the adventure: what lies on the other side! For others it's a clean start. For everyone (PAUSE) it's a clean start!

You're here tonight then you've thought about it. You're here tonight then you've read our literature, you've seen what we have to offer! I'm not going to give you some great spiel about how great we are, or how great LIFE is with us – how much better we are than our competitors!

No. It ain't about that! It's about you. What you want. What you want out of the experience.

A new start. A new start!

We're gonna be around here for a bit. Come talk to us. Come see what we have to say. No hard sell, no deadlines, no missed opportunities!

A new start! A new LIFE!

And all we need for a new LIFE... is a new door.

Come talk to us. There's refreshments at the back. Anything you want to know we're here for you. Thank you for listening and have a good night.

Thank you.

EXITS TO APPLAUSE.

Thank you very much.

FADE TO BLACK.

END OF ACT 1.

THE RECRUITMENT OFFICER

ACT 2

ACT 2

SCENE 1

THE HALL AFTERWARDS. TOM IS SITTING AT A DESK WITH A YOUNG RECRUIT WHO IS SIGNING PAPERS.

MALE 1   (REFERRING TO THE PAPERS) Here?

TOM   At the bottom as well. You smoke?

MALE 1   No.

TOM   Mind if I do? Terrible habit I know, but it takes the years off.

MALE 1   I'm, um, I'm asthmatic?!

TOM   Guess I'd better not then.

MALE 1   (FINISHING) And that's it then?

TOM   That's it.

MALE 1   (RELIEVED) I… phew… it's just… I've done anything like this before.

TOM   No, no, a lot of us don't! Takes guts. Not a lot of guys have that. Congratulations.

TOM EXTENDS A HAND AND MALE 1 SHAKES. HE LAUGHS.

MALE 1   I can't believe… wow.

TOM   You're doing just great!

MALE 1   What now?

TOM   You go through the door.

MALE 1   This one.

TOM   This very one.

MALE 1   Okay. Right.

TOM   Just take your time with it.

THEY MOVE OVER TO THE DOOR.

ENTER JULIA.

JULIA ENTERS AND WATCHES.

MALE 1   Did your dad make this one?

TOM   Everything you want to know is on the other side.

MALE 1   You're not coming.

TOM   Doesn't work that way. This is your door! Your LIFE! Ain't no one can go through it but you!

MALE 1   Right.

TOM   Don't forget to breathe, alright?

MALE 1   Ha. Alright.

HE LETS OUT A DEEP BREATH AND TAKES THE HANDLE.

MALE 1   I can't come back, can I?

TOM   It's all you.

MALE 1   (SUDDENLY SOMBRE) Good.

HE OPENS THE DOOR AND STEPS THROUGH, DISAPPEARING ON THE OTHER SIDE.

TOM PUSHES THE DOOR SHUT.

HE LOOKS AT HIS WATCH, AND STARTS TO GATHER UP THE PAPERS FROM THE TABLE.

JULIA   Is the accent real?

TOM   Ma'am?

JULIA   The accent, is it real?

TOM   Are you interested in joining one of…

JULIA   No! No, I'm just… I'm the manager. Of the centre. That was very impressive.

TOM   He's a good kid. He'll do well.

JULIA   I meant the speech.

TOM   Well, thank you. And, yes. The accent is real.

JULIA   I just thought… It's… right? You know? Some accents… You couldn't be a Welsh art curator could you? Wouldn't work! (IN WELSH ACCENT) Matisse's blue period. (REVERTING) It just… well, it's… you have the right accent for the job.

TOM   I don't think Matisse had a blue period.

JULIA   No, I don't think so either. (EXTENDING A HAND) I'm Julia.

TOM   Yes, ma'am. I'm Tom.

JULIA   (ENJOYING THE SOUND) Tom.

TOM   Thank you for the use of the facilities.

JULIA   You rented them.

TOM   Yes, ma'am.

JULIA   Do you do it a lot? The speech, I mean, it's very good. You're very good at it.

TOM   It's just talking, ma'am.

JULIA   Every day?

TOM   (SMILING) No. I… I guess I do it about twice a week. Not the same speech, you know? You've got to pick your audience. Tell them what they want to hear.

JULIA   And it's good? The job, I mean, not, you know, empirically?

TOM   Would you like to get coffee?

JULIA   I have to close up.

TOM   Yes ma'am. I'll get out of your way.

JULIA   (SITTING) It doesn't… I don't know… it all seems a bit, well… playing on people's emotions?

TOM   (SITTING AS WELL) How'd you mean?

JULIA   I don't know, I mean; the sell? You do it very well and everything.

TOM   Listen, I… I been doing this some time and if I've learnt one thing: you can't sell no one nothing they don't want. Anyway, this isn't selling.

JULIA   What is it?

TOM   Recruitment.

JULIA   Feels like conversion!

TOM   (LAUGHING) No, ma'am.

JULIA   Little bit.

TOM   No, ma'am.

JULIA   I like the 'ma'ams'.

TOM   Yes, 'ma'am'. This isn't… what did you call

it?

JULIA   Conversion.

TOM   No, this isn't conversion! This isn't selling, neither. I recruit! Nothing more, nothing less. People want change. They don't want to be stagnant…

JULIA   Yeah, but the people you work for…

TOM   Are good people! They are! They believe in their work, sure, but there's nothing shameful about that! Haven't you ever just wanted to… end 'it'? Just looked around the room; maybe even this room, and just said to yourself; "I can't be here no more!" Really? Look me in the eyes and tell me you've never thought about that and… why, I'll quit right now! Here on the spot! We all get to the point some time or another. Can't go on like this forever. Some of us dismiss it, push it down, soldier on, some just up and say enough. Not going to do it. Simple as that. (PAUSE) What you folks put on here usually anyway?

JULIA   It's a theatre!

TOM   Hmm, escapism! Ain't no one going to buy into that! (THEY SMILE) You want dinner? I ain't eaten and it's sure better eating with company than eating alone.

JULIA   I've got to lock up.

TOM   Well, I'll get out of your hair, then.

JULIA   Yeah, I probably…

TOM   You change your mind I'm at the hotel on Westbury? Couple of blocks over. In case you get hungry like.

JULIA   Sorry to have disturbed you.

TOM   No. It was nice meeting you, Julia. Hope to
do it again. Goodbye.

TOM EXITS. JULIA WAITS, THINKS, THEN GOING
ACROSS TO THE WALL, TURNS THE LIGHTS OFF.

SCENE 2

MALE 1   I think I was... maybe eleven, twelve? Something like that, I'm not really sure. But; I was young, I know that, when I first thought about it. It's... There's a... I don't know. The world is a big place; to a kid, a big place and I guess I just thought about... that maybe it would be better if, you know, I could make it smaller.

What we are... what happens around us is... well, it's pretty much the same thing, isn't it? I mean, again and again? The same thing, that's what I was thinking. What I've always thought I guess and, I mean, I didn't really do that well at school and I know that's not supposed to matter or anything and I don't think it stops anyone but... I could see it, you know. I could just see it out there, waiting for me? The same thing as my parents, same thing as my grandparents and not, you know, like there's anything wrong with that, for them, but...

Anyway, by the time I hit twenty I... Well, I was pretty much into drugs which, you know, is fine and everything and it wasn't, you know, it was just recreational and... fun. A lot of it. Very fun some of it, but even that gets old after a while so I, you know, stopped.

You get to that certain age, don't you? That age... and I think it's different for different people but that age where it's all just too much really. Just... And I don't know what to say about that, so I stopped drugs, or, at least, not as much as I used to and there was this girl... well, not this girl... Ellie. Her name was Ellie and it went really well for a while and then really shit: can I say 'shit'? Because, well, that's what it went.

So you know, school, drugs, women: shit. And you start to see a pattern, don't you? I mean, no matter how thick you are you start to notice things; trends! Everything starts great. Starts are great. Starts are frankly the best thing that's happened to you and then it goes bad, sometimes slowly, sometimes... (CLICKS FINGERS)

And, I mean, you notice. You just... Work... (PAUSE) So you notice and you notice that all these things, all these things, they start great and go shit and the only constant is: you. You! You're the only fucking thing they have in common. Good to bad and no matter what you try to do you just don't seem to be able to break the cycle so, in the end, you think... why bother with the starts in the first place?

I guess... for me, well the last one, the last start... I was... I don't know what it was, you know what I mean? I'd changed jobs, changed relationships. I was living with this girl and it was... it 'was', you know?! And she wasn't like, the one, or anything like that but she was, in every way imaginable pretty fucking great and we'd moved into this house, I mean not far from the centre and I was working in this hospital doing admin and, you know, there's not really much you can say other than it was going about as well as it had ever gone.

Which I guess is why I decided to end it just... Good times. And I'd got them about as small as they could get and... the cycle... So I got the pills from the hospital, which was easy enough, and just ended it. Then and there. Ran a bath and just got it all over with.

You don't have any more starts, you can't have any more

endings. That's just how it is really.

SCENE 3

A RESTAURANT.

TOM IS SITTING AT A TABLE, EATING AND READING. JULIA WALKS IN, WRAPPED UP WARM.

SHE SEES TOM BEFORE HE SEES HER, MAKES HER WAY OVER TO THE TABLE AND SITS.

JULIA   It's freezing out there.

TOM   (PLEASED AND SURPRISED) Hi. Yes, yes it is.

JULIA   Have you eaten? I'm not really hungry but if you haven't eaten.

TOM   I've eaten.

JULIA   I'll just get coffee then. (SHE LOOKS AROUND) Hello?! (TO TOM) Is anyone actually working here?

TOM   How was the theatre?

JULIA   What do you mean?

TOM   Closing it? Were there any problems?

JULIA   No! No. Sales conferences are much easier than theatre audiences. I don't know what it is about theatre shows, maybe it's the money, maybe it's the acting, but people think it's their divine right to never find a bin at the end of a show. Sales conference audiences… is that the right word? Audiences? Sales conference audiences are a lot neater. That or they don't eat, anyway.

TOM   Maybe it's the alcohol. We don 't encourage them to drink during the presentations.

JULIA   In theatre it's the only way to stop them leaving at the interval. Anyway; maybe you'd be more successful if you let them. Drink.

TOM   We're pretty successful at the moment.

JULIA   Yes, you are, aren't you. So this is your life, is it? One town to another? One country to another?! LIFE on the road.

TOM   This is my life.

JULIA   And you like it? I'd think it'd get pretty tedious.

TOM   (LEANING FORWARD) Where you from, Julia?

JULIA   I thought it was 'ma'am'.

TOM   'Ma'am' is for work. This here's my off time.

JULIA   I liked the 'ma'am'.

TOM   Where you from, ma'am?

JULIA   Here.

TOM   Just here.

JULIA   Where else?

TOM   And you've never want to go 'there', at all?

JULIA   Not really, no. Why?

TOM   Because, ma'am… Julia. I think you'd like it. I think you're itching to know… something. Something else.

JULIA SMILES.

JULIA   That the best you got?

TOM   I'm sorry?

JULIA   I honestly can't tell if that was a pick-up line or a sales pitch.

TOM   It was an observation.

JULIA   Well, Tom, what if I'm not? What if I'm not looking for 'something'. 'Something else'.

TOM   Then I'd say I was a very unlucky man, ma'am.

PAUSE. THEY'RE ENJOYING EACH OTHER.

JULIA   Where are you from?! I can't… I imagine you living on some great plantation somewhere, waking up to the sounds of workers in the field. I bet you wear white suits, don't you?

TOM   I put my shoes on one at a time, just like everyone else.

JULIA   Is it exciting? The travelling, I mean?

TOM   It has its moments.

JULIA   And those stories, the ones you told about your daddy…

TOM   Total bullshit, I assure you.

JULIA   (LAUGHING) Ha! I knew it!

TOM   It's my job.

JULIA   I knew it!

TOM   Fact of the matter is, I don't have the faintest who my daddy was. Mother neither. I am what I am. Maybe that's what I'm doing here, who's to tell!

JULIA   You know I grew up just around the corner from here.

TOM   That a fact?

JULIA   That is. A fact. Yes, it is! I grew up just around the corner from here, got my friends here, got my life here.

TOM   And now you manage the local theatre.

JULIA   (IRKED) It's hardly local.

TOM   No, I didn't mean.

JULIA   It's pretty 'West End' really. For here.

TOM   I meant no disrespect.

JULIA   Fact of the matter is I started working there because... well, I don't know. It was bigger, wasn't it? Theatre. Different worlds, different imaginings. I wanted to see things but I didn't want to leave.

TOM   And now you're manager.

JULIA   And now I'm the manager.

TOM   Who picks up litter and locks up after the guests?

JULIA   They're hardly guests. And no. As a matter of fact, we have interns for that. I... supervise them.

THEY BOTH LAUGH.

JULIA   (CONT.) Alright, it's not the greatest job in the world, but I like it. I get to see shows for free and I get to meet different people, people from other walks of life and… shows, I get to see shows.

TOM   Have dinner with interesting salesmen…

JULIA   Are you interesting?

TOM   You're still here, aren't you?

JULIA   Why are there never any waiters in this place?

TOM   I just kind of fell into it really. The job. I've, well I've done just about every sales job under the sun and you can imagine, there's really only so much that's different with them but life… I don't know, this one is different. This, and I know you may think differently, but this is not a hard sell! I get to meet different people, interesting people and we do, clichéd as it sounds, we do get to help a lot of folk work through a lot of things. And we're growing!

JULIA   Wow.

TOM   What?

JULIA   No, you just… wow, you really sound like the brochure!

TOM   Am I that bad?

JULIA   Just a little.

TOM   I'm sorry.

JULIA   No, it's… well, we don't do happy. We don't. Really. Not here. If we're lucky we get mildly pissed off but happy, contented? That we don't get. Not really. It's just not who we are.

TOM   You make it sound so appealing!

JULIA   Yes, I suppose I do. Listen, I… I think I'd

better go.

TOM   Alright.

JULIA   There's a… The waiter's not going to…
and I've got work tomorrow.

TOM   Same place, same time.

JULIA   That's right.

TOM   Have dinner with me.

JULIA   I… Thank you. I don't know.

TOM   I can promise you; there may even be
waiters.

JULIA   You're leaving: town.

TOM   At the end of the week.

JULIA   Yes, but… you're still leaving.

TOM   True, but, and there's no real way of getting
away from this but… I may want to have dinner before
that and, I don't know what passes for service in this town,
maybe it's how you keep yourselves in shape, but maybe
you will too.

JULIA   Alright.

TOM   It's just dinner.

JULIA   Tomorrow. After the show.

TOM   Not a show.

JULIA   (SMILING AGAIN) I… no. Sorry. Force
of habit. Tomorrow, after the conference.

TOM   I'll look forward to it.

JULIA   Goodnight.

TOM   (EXTENDING A HAND) It's nice to meet you, miss. Julia.

JULIA   Ma'am.

TOM   Ma'am.

JULIA   I swear that accent's fake! Goodnight.

TOM   Goodnight to you. Ma'am.

JULIA LEAVES AND TOM TURNS TO THE TABLE TO LOOK AT THE BILL, FIDDLING THROUGH HIS POCKETS FOR THE RIGHT MONEY.

DAVE ENTERS AND BRUSHES PAST JULIA. CLEARLY AGITATED HE MAKES HIS WAY OVER TO THE TABLE AND TOM.

DAVE   (TO JULIA) Sorry.

JULIA   (TO DAVE) Excuse me.

DAVE   (REACHING THE TABLE) There you are.

TOM   (WITHOUT LOOKING UP) David. It's so good to see you again.

DAVE   Can the southern charm shit. Been looking for you everywhere.

TOM   Can this wait until morning? It's been quite a long day. The conference was good, if you're interested.

DAVE SITS, THEN HALF STANDS.

DAVE   No, it can't. What you got to do to get some service in this place?

TOM   Become a waiter, it would seem.

TOM WEARILY SITS AGAIN.

DAVE   Fuck it! What were you saying about the conference?

TOM   It went well. Good turnout. Great response. I'm not entirely sure…

DAVE   How many?

TOM   I'm not entirely…

DAVE   How many?!

TOM   Is that what it's about, Dave?

DAVE   Of course it's what it's fucking about 'Tom'. We're a fucking recruitment company, not a literary fucking wank fest. What did you think it was about?

TOM   People, Dave. I was under the strange misconception this was about people. At least that's what I've been out telling whoever will listen.

DAVE   Do I look like I give a fuck about people, Tom? Do I look like I give a shit about my fellow man, because I'd hate to think you was labouring under a miscompre-fucking-hension! If I'm coming across, or have ever come across as if I give a flying fuck about absolutely anyone but me and mine, then I want you to tell me because, obviously, I'm not dressing for the occasion. Now, how fucking many did you recruit?

TOM   Twelve.

DAVE   Twelve!

TOM   I think…

DAVE   I don't give a fuck what you think 'twelve'! I don't give a fuck! Out of how many 'twelve'?

TOM   Little over two hundred.

DAVE   Twelve!!!

TOM   Which is over five per cent, which is…

DAVE   Five percent, five fucking percent you're coming at me with? Am I listening to this?!

TOM   (TRYING TO CALM HIMSELF) Dave… it's the first day. Twelve is fine. Twelve is above average. The numbers will roll, they always do. We got a near full house, now, that's something! It is! On the first day, that's something! Twelve is good. We're still on target for the week and I think we're going to surprise you with…

DAVE   Well, you're gonna fucking have to, aren't you!

TOM   I'm sorry?

DAVE   You're gonna fucking have to! Surprise me? You're gonna fucking have to!

PULLING A PIECE OF PAPER FROM HIS POCKET.

DAVE   You know what I have here?

TOM   Listen, it's late, why don't we get breakfast…

DAVE   Global numbers! Right here. And we're down! Right fucking here!

TOM   I think you'll find we're not!

DAVE   Two.

TOM   Two? Two is not a decrease…

DAVE   Of course it's not a fucking decrease, but it is a slow. A slow. And the projections…

TOM   We're… David. LIFE… We're the best recruiting agency in the world. The best! That's why you hired me. Now, okay. We're not the States. We're not China. We don't want to be! You hired me because of what I can do; so let me do it. Our numbers are fine! They're just fine! People don't want to change! They're not asking themselves; 'what for' that much anymore. They've got their interests and they're…

DAVE   Ten years. Ten years, that's what they pay me for! Point fucking three percent increase in over ten years. Thirty years recruitment was down, thirty fucking years and then, last ten, up point three fucking percent! You know what that is in numbers? No, neither do I, but that's where we fucking are and you're going to give me 'inter-fucking-rests'.

TOM   Five percent is a good showing!

DAVE   Five percent is a fucking doddle. Five percent my mother can get in. Fuck, stick on an open stage and five percent are going to walk through the door out of sheer fucking boredom! You got five days, Tom. Five fucking days and if we're not seeing two hundred new recruits by fucking then then you're gonna fuck off back to the cotton pickers and fuck the lot of you!

DAVE GETS UP TO LEAVE.

DAVE   Five fucking percent! Where'd you read that? Back of a fucking cereal packet?! And get another tie, for fuck's sake. This is England, not the Gone With The Fuckwind. Five fucking percent! Get some sleep, Tom.

Tomorrow your fucking daddy's gonna have to do better than a fucking door maker!

EXIT DAVE.

LIGHTS DOWN ON TOM.

SCENE 4

LIGHTS UP ON FEMALE 1.

FEMALE 1   I met him… through friends, I suppose, thought I can't actually tell you any of their names anymore which, I suppose, is a little strange but that's what life does to you, doesn't it? What's important, what's not?

We were married twelve months later. All our friends. Even those I've forgotten, I suppose. If I had the photos in front of me… but there we go. It was a lovely ceremony. Not the best of weather and there was a little problem with the chairs but I had the dress I wanted and the man as well.

It's strange. I wasn't, actually, in love with him at this point. I thought I was, of course, but actually I was still in love with, well, someone else, but I thought I was. It's strange how that works. I think it wasn't until Ian was born that I realized… until I became, completely and utterly, insanely in love with him. A shocking thing to imagine but there we are, I suppose.

Ian was born, eight-thirty, eighth of August. A little ditty for us to remember him by. Not the easiest birth. (PAUSE) Not the easiest year, either. I… It's a hard thing to hate your own child. A hard thing. I loved him, of course, but I could tell, from the love I'd just discovered for my husband that I didn't 'love' him. (PAUSE) I hated him.

It was that way for about the first two years, I think. Just over. I resented… it's hard for me to say this now, of course, looking back… Looking back I think; 'how could you have felt that way about something that precious? How could you?' But that's how it was. I used to… cry, when he'd cry. When Andrew wasn't around. I'd just hold him and cry. (JOKING) Who could cry the loudest. (SADLY) And I'd... I'd shake him as well. Too hard, really.

Postnatal depression, that's what they called it. But it doesn't matter what they call it, does it. It matters what it is. Understanding it doesn't make it something else, does it.

Perhaps I love late? I'd never thought about that. Andrew, my husband. Ian. It wasn't until his second year... I mean, up to that I'd just go through the ropes. Just doing what mothers do. And sleeping. Sleeping. I slept a lot in those two years. Just, crying and sleeping. But after that... I think it was when he became a person! When he started to talk and learn things, I mean he was learning all the time but, really learn things, that I started to really love him. Like a mother should. Like I wanted to.

Six months later Abby came. Which, I have to tell you, frightened me. Seriously frightened me! I thought if this is the way it was with Ian - Andrew's father's name was Ian - if this is the way it was with Ian, how's it going to be this time? But it wasn't like that. It was great! Even the pregnancy. I mean, I still got sick and everything but it wasn't like it was with Ian.

She was born sixth of January. No mnemonics there and quite the little bitch she was from the outset, which is odd really, because Ian was always so placid. But you can't help but love her, you know? Just, all of them.

And then Scarlett, two years later. Scarlett had learning problems. She was – we didn't know this at the time - but she was deaf in one ear. Gave her problems with balance. Slightly autistic but it didn't matter. I mean, the autism, that was tough, you know, but the kids loved her! And Andrew was so good with her, you know what I mean?

And it's… They were golden years really. Ten, fifteen of them. Golden years. We weren't well off or anything and Andrew worked all hours but we were, happy. As corny as it sounds, we were happy.

And then Ian moved away to university. He's a lawyer. Came home every holiday. And then Abby. Scarlett was more problematic. She stayed with us for thirty years. She got that 'assisted housing' in the end. But she was never far from us.

How did I ever not love him? I ask myself that. All the time. How did I ever not love him?

There was a rough patch. Just after the two moved out, I was given cancer. Strange how you think of it like that, but that's how it was. And it was hard on Andrew.

We were still young, you see. When the kids moved out. Barely forty and I think he thought there'd be time for us, even with Scarlett, but I was given cancer. Ovarian. Far too early. And that all died for us.

LIGHTS UP IN THE AUDITORIUM.

IN SEMI DARKNESS TOM IS RECRUITING THE SAME WOMAN AT A YOUNGER AGE.

THEY TALK, SHE SIGNS. SHE IS CLEARLY UPSET. WIPING TEARS FROM HER EYES. TOM LEADS HER TO THE DOOR. SHE HUGS HIM. HE OPENS IT AND SHE STEPS THROUGH.

We used to take Scarlett out to the cliffs, you know. So she could feel the wind and everything. We used to take her out there and I can still see him now. Hands in pockets. Stoic. That little bit of grey in the temples that I used to play with. That openness…

He died fourteen days after my sixty-third. Got given cancer too, though we didn't know it. One week he was fine, bit of back pain, next he was gone.

Scarlett was in a home by then, of course, but they all came back. Even Abby. Because I loved him, see? Totally loved him. And when he died; everything was minus him. The kitchen. Toilet seat. Cliffs. Just… so, painful, you know?

I kept hearing from the kids, of course. Ian even moved his practice to look after me. Brought the grandkids with him. Abby finally settled down. Well, for Abby. And she calls when there's a problem.

Scarlett even got a fella.

And even then, they weren't bad times. I missed him. I did. All the way. But the grandkids and watching everyone grow and get on with their lives… I loved that.

I don't remember passing away. I guess it would be strange if I did. So, the only thing I can tell you is that I remember getting up in the morning. I was expecting Scarlett's fella for the afternoon. He was coming to do some work on the spare bedroom. We'd converted it for Abby's oldest's boy when she ran out on him, but he'd moved on to the city now, done something with a charity organization or something and Steve was coming round to make it, well, less, eighteen year old boy, I suppose. Bit of paint, nothing more.

Good kids, all of them. Very proud of them.

But I suppose I never got there, because I know I needed to leave the spare key under the mat for him and I know I never got round to it.

Such good kids. And I loved him. All of them. All of it, really. When you think of it like that.

And that's not bad when you come to think about it. Life. Really is worth it.

Change is as good as a rest.

FADE TO BLACK.

END OF ACT 2.

ACT 3

ACT 3

SCENE 1

LIGHTS UP ON THE AUDITORIUM.

TOM IS SHAKING HANDS WITH A COUPLE OF PEOPLE AT THE CLOSE OF A SESSION. THEY'RE NOT SIGNING UP BUT THEY DO SEEM TO BE FANS.

TOM   Well, thank you.

MALE 2   And Cincinnati.

FEMALE 2   Though you were better in New York.

TOM   Ain't that nice of you!

MALE 2   Just the biggest fans!

TOM   Don't forget to sign up, now!

FEMALE 2   Oh, we will.

MALE 2   We will.

TOM   (JOKING) Pull the band-aid off as my daddy used to say!

MALE 2   We will!

FEMALE 2   We loved you in Cincinnati!

TOM   London loves you too!

FEMALE 2   We're not there, yet!

TOM   I understand.

MALE 2   It's a journey.

TOM   It is.

MALE 2   You were wonderful in New York.

TOM   Well, alrighty now.

FEMALE 2   We are so excited for when it's our time.

TOM   You folks take care now!

MALE 2   I loved the new material!

TOM   You take care.

THEY MOVE TO LEAVE.

ENTER JULIA.

FEMALE 2   You're the best.

TOM   Go safely now, you hear!

MALE 2   And we've seen all of them!

JULIA   I didn't know you had groupies!

SHE MOVES OVER AND KISSES HIM ON THE
CHEEK. THEY ARE TENDER.

TOM   I swear! Comes with the territory, I'm
afraid. I thought you were off tonight.

JULIA   I swapped. You were good tonight. Different.

TOM   You were watching?

JULIA   I wanted to see what all the fuss was about.

TOM   It's not a performance.

JULIA   Of course it is!

TOM   Well, not that kind of performance, anyway!

JULIA   Yeah, but… every salesman has their stichik,
right? Their patter. Lines. It's all very theatrical.

TOM   So does every believer. Every pick-up artist!

JULIA   Is that what you are?

TOM   Hardly! I had a great time last night.

JULIA GOES OVER TO THE DOOR.

JULIA   So this is it, huh?

TOM   (JOKING) The one my father made.

JULIA   How does it work?

TOM   I couldn't even begin to tell you.

SHE WALKS AROUND THE DOOR.

JULIA   They just walk through it and… whoosh!
Off they go?

TOM   That's about it.

JULIA   In one side, out on another.

TOM   In one side, out nowhere.

JULIA   Like a magic trick?

TOM   Like a, as you say, magic trick.

JULIA   What does it look like?

TOM   What do you mean?

JULIA   Well, you've seen it. You open the door for
them. You close it. What does it look like? Through the
door.

TOM   (SHRUGGING) It's just… light.

JULIA   Light?

TOM   Nothing more, nothing less. Really bright

light. I keep my eyes closed most of the time.

JULIA   That's not you doing that?

TOM   How do you mean?

JULIA   I thought that was all stagecraft, you know. The light. You wouldn't have thought it would be like that.

TOM   No stagecraft, I assure you.

JULIA PULLS THE DOOR OPEN SUDDENLY AND LOOK DISAPPOINTED. SHE STEPS THROUGH AND APPEARS ON THE OTHER SIDE.

JULIA   It's not on.

TOM   I guess not.

JULIA   How does that work?

JULIA SEEMS DISAPPOINTED. TOM IS UNCOMFORTABLE AND MOVES OVER TO THE DESK.

JULIA   And you've never been tempted?

TOM   Come again?

JULIA   You've never been tempted to just, I don't know, walk through. Go yourself. I don't know! Tempted!

TOM   Not in the slightest!

JULIA   That seems strange, doesn't it? A salesman not trying his own wares.

TOM   If I tried it, I wouldn't be able to sell it.

JULIA   Yeah, but still, you've never been tempted.

TOM   Where do you want to eat?

JULIA   I think I would. Be tempted.

TOM   It's a job, Julia. Nothing more, nothing less.

JULIA   I would though. If I was doing it day in, day out. I'd be tempted to just open the door for someone and then… step through myself.

TOM   I could eat a horse! Not metaphorical, actual!

JULIA   Maybe I'll sign up.

TOM   Don't even joke about it! Come on.

JULIA   No! Why not? If it's good enough for them.

TOM   LIFE… you get one go at LIFE. That's all. You walk through that door, that's it. No coming back.

JULIA   That's the appeal, surely!

TOM   It's…

JULIA   What?

TOM   It's for desperate people! People who can't be happy! Can't find an equilibrium. Can't settle.

JULIA   You don't settle.

TOM   I settle at not settling. That's what I do!

JULIA   (SHRUGGING) You sell something you don't believe in!

TOM   Look, I'm tired and I'm hungry, can we please…

JULIA   No, I mean, you know, that's not very nice, is it?! Selling something you don't believe in!

TOM   I do believe in it!

JULIA   You said…

TOM   …just not for everybody! Look! We're happy. I mean, aren't we happy? Right here, right now? This minute? This week? Maybe everyone should take it. Everyone should take the out! I don't know! At the right time, at their time of life. That's not for me to say. It's an option. Not everybody can be… 'contented'. But now, for me? Well, I'd be contented with a good steak, a fine bottle of wine and your beautiful company! So, if we can just get out of here…

JULIA   I'm sorry.

TOM   This is work, you know? And I'm not getting paid, so…

JULIA   You're right. I wasn't thinking.

THEY EXIT, HAND IN HAND. AT THE LAST MOMENT JULIA TURNS AND LOOKS AT THE DOOR.

SCENE 2

MALE 2   I don't give a shit about births and deaths and shit like that. No one does. We all get born, we all die. Talking about it innt gonna make it any easier. Suffice to say aye got into the prison life, pretty early. Dad had done a stint, some shit in a bar. Fucker said something to 'im an' 'e was off. Fine by me, like. Couldn't lock the bastard up enough, if you catch my drift.

Aye was firteen aye did my first stint inside. Some fucking car thing and I tried to give the pig something an' got my hide tanned for it.

In an' out from then on. Nah, you get used to it, you know? Aye knew blokes who'd rather do time than live on the outside, if you know what aye mean. Not that I was far off, mine. Got six for aggravated assault for the fucker who did my sister but there was this chimney in the block below me who liked to play the trombone so I gave him one right up his jacksie and that got turned into fifteen.

You know, there's a lot of shit talked about screws and tikers, an' most of it's bollocks, innit. Just, people, same as any other. You got your communities and your rules and what not and you just get on with it.

Fuck and don't get fucked on. Pretty much all you got in your life.

Take our Rita, right? Shacked up with this bloke, you know. Paki fucker. And the boys start givin' me agro about it, so I did 'im. Simple as. An' 'at's another twenty for you!

Ain't gonna have some Paki do up your eldest, no matter where he's from, right?

Nah, you get used to it, yeah. Fuck or get fucked on. An' you get used to it, right. Nah, the foods not exactly fucking Freud's but when it's all you got it's not so bad.

An' you get used to it. The aggro. The screws. Meatpackers. An' you get your mates an' they got you.

Cancer, though, that's another fing. How'd you get cancer in a fucking six by four? Six years I was in and out of hospital. Six years! Let me out in the end on compassion, they called it. Never even got to say goodbye to the lads, you know.

Spent me last months in Rita's back room with her Paki kids changing my skivvies. Used to show me! Pissing in my food. What sort of end is that?

Least with the boys you know where you are, alright.

SCENE 3

THE RESTAURANT. JULIA AND TOM ARE HAVING DINNER. THEY ARE BOTH HAPPY.

TOM   Six! I would have to say, from the world weary look behind your eyes, that you are a six.

JULIA   Six?

TOM   Not a moment sooner.

JULIA   Try seven-thirty.

TOM   Ah, the joys of working in a theatre!

JULIA   Who gets up before six?

TOM POINT TO HIMSELF WITH HIS FORK.

JULIA   Before six?

TOM   Five-thirty at the latest!

JULIA   That's just sadism.

TOM   It is in this country! When does your sun rise!? I been whole days without seeing its face!

JULIA   Alright, my turn.

TOM   Go right ahead.

JULIA   Dog.

TOM   Yes.

JULIA   Boxers rather than briefs.

TOM   How right you are!

JULIA   And… doughnuts over bagels.

TOM   Oooh. How close you were!

JULIA   Really?

TOM   Bagel is god's gift, ma'am. Doughnut is Satan's a-hole.

THEY LAUGH.

JULIA   I used to think, when I was young…

TOM   Not anymore?

JULIA   America is not a real place, is it? Not really. I used to… When you get on an airplane, when you're travelling, not that I did travel, mind you. My parents were not what you would call 'travellers'. But when you flew: to America. I believed they were faking it. Just… faking it. They'd run movies past the airplane windows or something and then, blam, you're in America! Only it wouldn't be America. It would be an aircraft hangar or something, full of actors. Actors with fake accents. Actors who… were there to make you believe you were in America, or something!

TOM   Why?

JULIA   Oh, I don't know. Soda fountains, I suppose. I remember hearing about them, when I was a girl. I remember hearing about them and… I suppose I didn't understand them. Not really. I used to believe they were actual soda fountains. In the middle of the square. For everyone to drink out of. Sponsored no doubt by some company or other. And the cars! 'Al-oo-min-e-um!' You had your own special metal! Lighter than… well, ours. It just didn't sound real, you know? So I thought they were making it up.

TOM   No, ma'am.

JULIA   America shouldn't be real.

TOM   It's exactly like here.

JULIA   I'm sure it is.

TOM   Towns… people.

JULIA   Right! Just like us, 'ma'am'!

TOM   I mean it. Everywhere's the same. People, I suppose. People are the same. The world over. You move enough and… well, that's just how it is. Same thing, same town. I don't think we're built for it. Change. Sometimes… one of the things I say in the presentations; we're supposed to be like butterflies. But we don't, fly. We're just caterpillars. Caterpillars that build our cocoons, weave them tightly around us and then… forget to come out again. And you know what? What's wrong with that?! Where's the beef? Sounds like a pretty decent life to me!

JULIA   You are so strange to me!

TOM   (MOTIONING TO HIS MOUTH) Do I have…

JULIA   No, I mean; in a good way! Strange! Different. New. I think I could listen to you all day.

TOM   Well, ma'am. We do try to please!

JULIA   It's just… Here you are… different. And… I didn't know I wanted different. I was… well, happy: no! Okay, not happy but… settled. And then there's you. You! And I just… There's a world out there, isn't there!? A whole world.

TOM   I don't want to…

JULIA   And it's the same. You're saying, exactly the same.

TOM   I don't know what you're driving at.

JULIA   Who wouldn't want to fly?

TOM   Maybe we could change the topic? (PAUSE) It's just that…

JULIA   No, of course!

TOM   It's work and…

JULIA   I completely understand.

TOM   I just find that I…

JULIA   It was rude of me.

TOM   No! It's…

JULIA   I understand.

PAUSE.

TOM   I like you and…

JULIA   Salted or sweet?

TOM   I'm sorry?

UNSEEN BY EITHER OF THEM DAVE ENTERS THE RESTAURANT. HE'S ABOUT TO PASS BY WHEN HE SEES THEM AND STOPS.

JULIA   Popcorn. Salted or sweet?

TOM   Salted. I… Potatoes or chips?

JULIA   My chips or your chips?

TOM   What are your chips?

JULIA   Crisps.

TOM   As in a note?

DAVE   Well, fuck me! Tom!

JULIA   Hello!

TOM   Why, David. Hello…

DAVE   (SITTING) Fancy bumping into you here! You don't mind do you, love? Hate eating alone?

TOM   Julia, this is David… Dave… Dave is area supervisor…

DAVE   Regional, sweetheart. Regional.

TOM   And this is Julia.

DAVE   Business dinner?

JULIA   I run the theatre you're renting.

DAVE   For the conference!? You sly fucking dog!

TOM   We're old friends.

DAVE   Where you from then, love?

JULIA   Here.

DAVE   (WITH IRONY AT TOM'S STATEMENT) Yeah? Me too.

TOM   I think perhaps…

JULIA   So you're his boss.

TOM   Well now…

DAVE   That's right love!

TOM   I think perhaps…

JULIA   So, you know how it works then. Tom, won't tell me.

DAVE   How what works, love?

JULIA   The door.

TOM   Don't you have…

DAVE   The door?

TOM   This is not the place…

DAVE   You know, I'm a simple man me. Been walking around for god knows how long. Don't fly, don't fall, don't suddenly float off into space at a moment's fucking notice, if you'll pardon my French, and the thing of it is, I don't need to know how it works: it works! Worked yesterday, worked today, will probably work tomorrow.

JULIA   And you don't question that?

TOM   Dave…

DAVE   Look, no, hold on Tom, the lady was asking a question. Look, this man here. He's the recruitment officer, alright? It's what he likes. It's what he does! He's for the flowery words and feelings and all that. I'm a straight shooter. I don't got to know why or what or even 'if'. I just got to make sure we meet our quotas and that's all there is to it.

JULIA   And you're not tempted?

DAVE   Tempted?

JULIA   To join up yourself. Walk through the door.

DAVE   Nah, that's a one way ticket, love. We recruit for LIFE. That's the end of it! You go in, you don't come back. See, some people, they're not content with that. Maybe you're not!

TOM   David.

DAVE   Doesn't matter to me, one way or another. This; day in, day out. Doing what you do. That's good enough for you then that's all you need to know, isn't it? If it's not? Life! If you can't get on with being what you are. That's not good enough for you, then we provide the opportunity. Simple as that! Nothing fancy about it. Not everyone is cut out for the world around them. Not everyone is going to be okay with it. You're not? We offer you the opportunity for change. We're like the armed forces, 'cept you don't need no weapons training!

TOM   I think I'll call it a night.

DAVE   Need a word in your shell like.

JULIA   No, it's me that should go.

TOM   No.

JULIA   Really, it's been a long day and… (RISING) It was nice to meet you.

DAVE   Likewise.

EXIT JULIA.

DAVE   (WATCHING HER GO) Think you might have made a recruit there!

TOM   Leave her alone.

DAVE   Fuck did I do? No! I just wanted to say… Those are good numbers you're bringing in. For the week! Head office are tickled.

TOM   Sure.

DAVE   We make a good team, you and me!

TOM   Leave her alone!

DAVE   Fuck that! She wants to join! You can see it in her! Far be it from me to tell you your business but that woman is looking for a change.

TOM   No!

DAVE   It's not like we're the only gig in town!

TOM   I said no!

DAVE   Tom, Tom! Seen that look a thousand times. Million of them. Seen it on every face of every loved one we ever signed up. Every complaint we get, that's the face on them! Why'd you let them join, they ask me. Why'd you sign them up for LIFE? 'Cept that's not really what they're asking. That's not really what they're looking for! "Why'd they leave me?" That's what they're really asking. "Why wasn't I enough." I'll give you a word of advice. Same one I don't give them, if you catch my drift!? We don't own them. Any of them. They're not here for us. They're here for themselves. All of us! You think I ain't thought of joining? I've thought about it. Life!? New start? New beginning? Step through the door and it's all over, right? Same old, same old, never again! 'S fucking tempting is what it is! But you know what? Same old ain't so bad! I'm alright with it! You're alright with it! Maybe one day you won't be alright with it, maybe I won't. Maybe we'll both hold hands and step through the fucking door together, am I right? Maybe we won't. Don't mean they are alright with it. Don't mean we don't have to let them go. Forgive them. It weren't us, that's what I want to tell them; when they come in. Weren't us. It was them. And there's nothing we can do about it but let them go!

TOM   (RISING) You come near her and I'll kill you!

TOM EXITS.

DAVE   (CALLING AFTER) Tom! TOM!!! Head office are happy, you dumb fuck! (BEAT) You're just being selfish! (PAUSE) What the fuck is it with service around here?

SCENE 4

FEMALE 2   It's the stuff that you never do that gets you, you know? Jumping out of airplanes, sailing boats off the edge of the world, that kind of thing. I never learnt to drive. It's a little thing but I just didn't need it!

I used to watch those nature documentaries. You know the ones? What people like us used to use TVs for, really. And every time I saw them I used to think… what am I doing here for? Why am I not, I don't know, kayaking off the icebergs in Greenland or flying gliders off the Victoria Falls. What's Islington got that those don't.

Restaurants, naturally, but you don't think about that when you're watching it, do you? You just think: "wish I was there." "Wish I was that!"

I mean, it's silly, really. You go through all those years of education and for what? What do you do with it? Slightly better dinner conversation? I left Oxford I had… 'the biggest plans', you know. Work, travel. Marta Hari. All of it.

And what came of it? Job at the gallery, Daniel made partner and then it's all prams and shopping and eating in the right places, which, let's face it, is still better than eating in the wrong places.

And we did travel. Daniel got division in New York and we spent five years overlooking the park. And, (EXCITED) ah, the friends. You wouldn't believe it. Film stars and arts benefits.

I met Hawking once. Strange man. Bad teeth. But you could see it in him, you know? You could just see it!

Alice went to Harvard. Neil went to Kings, which, I wasn't

pleased about but Daniel insisted. And they did well. Alice moved to Shanghai with an investment bank and Neil is something in the music industry, though it's all a bit beyond me.

And we thrive. It's what we do, really. Thrive. I remember talking to Neil Young of all people and I remember thinking it strange because, for the life of me, I couldn't remember even one of his songs and then he said to me; change tracks. Simple as that. Change tracks. (THINKS) Quite out of the blue really.

After Daniel there was the charity work and the boards and I was still very interested in the arts.

Change tracks. (PAUSE) Smaller than you'd think, Neil Young. Always thought of him as a towering man but quite effete.

We lost Alice to a plane crash. One of those things, I suppose. And Neil did well enough though, I would have liked grandchildren. Still, that's the music industry for you, isn't it?

Took me three times to make it out. Could never stand the other ways and the problem with pills is that they are so slow to take, aren't they? All that one at a time. First two times I kept being found by the maid which, naturally, meant I had to keep changing maids, but I made it out eventually.

Ghastly thing, LIFE. We're quite unprepared for it, you know. No one ever tells you that. Quite unprepared. (IRONICALLY) Change tracks!

SCENE 5

IN THE AUDITORIUM, JULIA IS PUTTING OUT CHAIRS.

ENTER TOM.

TOM   Julia.

JULIA   Morning.

TOM   I tried to call you last night.

JULIA   Yeah, sorry about that. I was… I was tired, you know? Big day for you today!

TOM   I don't understand.

JULIA   Big push, last day and everything! Quite the crowd you've got out there.

TOM   About that. See, I've been thinking somewhat and…

JULIA   Is that enough chairs? They asked us to put chairs out.

TOM   (TAKING HER ARM) Enough. Alright. Enough. I want to talk.

JULIA   Well, I don't. So…

TOM   I'm thinking of staying.

JULIA   (PAUSE) Okay.

TOM   We're doing really well and…

JULIA   Can you do that?

TOM   I don't see why not.

JULIA   I…

TOM   Look, this week… It's been important to me. You understand? Important. You… are important. And I've liked being here with you, simple as that. And I'd like to be with you some more.

JULIA RAISES HER HANDS TO HIS FACE.

JULIA   You are so sweet. You know that?

TOM   Can I stay?

JULIA   You're asking me for permission?

TOM   Chivalry, all evidence to the contrary, is not dead!

JULIA   (PULLING AWAY) I'm not your mother.

TOM   I wasn't asking you to be!

JULIA   Felt a bit like it.

TOM   I just…

JULIA   I'm not… I… I've liked you too! Being here. It… You're sweet and you're charming and… it's made me realize some things. Some things I wasn't admitting to myself.

TOM   For example.

JULIA   I… I need a change. I need… something.

TOM   No.

JULIA   It's not…

TOM   Julia, listen to me! Nobody knows what happens in LIFE. Nobody! Not me, no matter what they tell you; nobody! This… this is not the answer! It's not! No one comes back, Julia, once you step through that door: no one comes back! We have no idea what happens in there. No one does and anyone who tells you any different is a liar! You understand?

JULIA   I just think…

TOM   You need change!?

JULIA   Yes.

TOM   This isn't enough?

JULIA   And you showed me that, you…

TOM   Then let me be that change! Let me help you change.

JULIA   What if you can't?

TOM   I can!

JULIA   I've been down this…

TOM   I can!

JULIA   Do you know what I thought. One week ago. Listening to you speak?

TOM   What?

JULIA   I thought… why are these people so unhappy? Why are they so… Why can't they just be satisfied with what they have, with what they've got?

TOM   I'm right here.

JULIA   And then I met you.

TOM   I don't know what to say to you.

JULIA   (LAUGHS) Well, I guess I have that going for me.

TOM   Let me be the change.

JULIA   Once you've turned the light on…

TOM   We'll talk. After this! We'll. Meet me here! After, and we'll talk. I promise. Just talk. Please. Ma'am.

JULIA   (LAUGHING) Ma'am! Sure. Sure! Alright. Here. After. You go give your speech and I'll be here. When you get back.

TOM   We'll talk. I promise.

JULIA   Go give your speech.

TOM   Right here.

JULIA   Right here.

TOM EXITS OUT THROUGH THE AUDIENCE.

JULIA GOES OVER AND RUNS HER HANDS ACROSS THE DOOR FRAME.

ENTER DAVE.

DAVE ENTERS, PAPERS IN HAND.

DAVE   You ready then?

JULIA   I think so.

DAVE   Best thing you've ever done.

JULIA   Is it painful.

DAVE   Absolutely   not.   Guaranteed   in   the paperwork, love.

JULIA   You wouldn't know though, right? I mean, if no one comes back.

DAVE   (SMILING)   No   one's   ever   made   a

complaint, right enough there.

JULIA   LIFE. It's a strange name. LIFE.

DAVE   Just got to get the paperwork out of the way.

JULIA   (COMING OVER TO THE TABLE) Will you tell him something for me?

THE TWO FALL INTO SILENCE AS TOM ENTERS ANOTHER PART OF THE STAGE AND BEGINS HIS SPEECH TO THE WAITING RECRUITS.

WHILE HE SPEAKS, JULIA SIGNS THE PAPERS AND DAVE LEADS HER OVER TO THE DOOR.

TOM   Ladies and gentlemen! Thank you all for waiting and thank you all for coming back! You're here tonight it's because you expressed an interest in joining us, but, whether it's because the time wasn't right for you, or you wanted some time to say goodbye, you haven't yet, and that's alright. That's alright!

You're here tonight and you should give yourselves a big hand. Come on!

TOM CLAPS AND ENCOURAGES EVERYONE TO DO THE SAME.

TOM   (CONT.) Yes, thank you. It's been an amazing week for us, yes it has and we're going to crack open the champagne in just a moment but before we do, I just want to share a few thoughts.

I get asked... a lot... I get asked three things. One, what are you doing on this side of the pond, to which I answer; I just can't get enough of your damn weather! That's right!

But the second question I get asked is; how do I know when I'm ready?

That's right! That's what we're all asking ourselves, right now!

Well, let me tell you. Life has a way of creeping up on you, yes it does. It has a way of finding you, just when you're not expecting it. Sometimes in a good way – and I've known many of them. Many! But sometime in a bad way as well.

So let me tell you. You know how you know when you're ready? When you're really ready? When you're ready to take that final step into LIFE?

When it's okay to let go. When it's in your heart to just let it all go.

JULIA TURNS AT THE DOOR AND SHAKES HANDS WITH DAVE. BREATHING DEEPLY SHE NODS AND HE OPENS THE DOOR.

SHE IS BATHED IN WHITE LIGHT AND STEPS THROUGH, DISAPPEARING. DAVE CLOSES THE DOOR.

TOM   (CONT.) The third question I get asked is; am I ever coming back? And… I don't have the answer for that one. That is between you and your god. Nothing I can say to it!

Maybe you've already been back. Maybe this is you on your way back through, these… are not the questions for a recruitment officer. I know only three things. You know that in your heart! You know that in your beliefs! You know it's time, time to be okay with letting go. Time to be okay with change, and I want you to say that with me. I know you can't out loud because you're British and everything, but I want you to say it in your hearts; it's okay to let go.

And lastly, and most importantly; I know one more thing. It's champagne time!

Make yourselves at home, talk to our reps and enjoy the evening. Thank you all for coming and good night!

LIGHTS DOWN ON TOM TO APPLAUSE.

SCENE 6

DAVE IS AT THE TABLE, GATHERING THE PAPERWORK.

ENTER TOM.

DAVE   Well, that went well!

TOM   Is that the numbers?

DAVE   I think I can safely say, for a one week conference that's about the best I've ever seen.

TOM   And what's our total?

DAVE   Pretty much near four, fuck you very much!

TOM   Well, that's just great. Really!

DAVE   (DUBIOUS) Oh, yeah?

TOM   I'm serious. A man must have pride in his work!

DAVE   (IRONICALLY) Glad you're finally coming around.

TOM   So, I've been thinking.

DAVE   That right?

TOM   You and me make quite the team and I'm thinking, what with all the interest we've generated over the last week, how about I stay on – hear me out – work out of the office for a few weeks, following up on leads, while we set up another conference. This time bigger. This time we really go for it. See if we can't get those numbers up before the winter. Big push kind of thing. What do you think?

DAVE SITS BACK AND LOOKS AT THE PAPERS IN FRONT OF HIM, THINKING.

DAVE   I think that's a great idea.

TOM   I thought you would!

DAVE   Yeah, you stay the fuck on and fuck your way through the support staff, why not!

TOM   Don't talk to me like that, now!

DAVE   Get over it, man. She's gone. And if you spent half as much energy getting recruits as you spent getting your end away we'd have pushed a thousand.

TOM   What do you mean she's 'gone'?

DAVE   I mean she's gone. Gone! LIFE! Gone! Got the paperwork right here to prove it.

HE GOES TO SHOW TOM THE PAPERWORK BUT IS ATTACKED BY TOM WHO GRABS HIM BY THE NECK AND LIFTS HIM OUT OF HIS CHAIR.

TOM   (ROARING) Tell me you are lying! Tell me you're lying!

DAVE   Fuck you! Think you're the only recruiter here!

TOM   You're a lying sack of shit!

DAVE   I was sleeping with you, I'd want to end it all as well!

TOM LETS OUT ANOTHER ROAR AND DRAGS THE MAN TOWARD THE DOOR.

DAVE   (CONT.) It's LIFE, Tom? It's… it's shitty and it's horrible but that's LIFE! No one can… no one can change, Tom! It's a cycle, nothing more! If it's not for… If it's not in us, it's just not in us! Listen to me, listen to me, you fucker! It would have ended! You would have left! You always leave. That's just what you do, for Christ's sake.

WITH A FINAL ROAR TOM OPENS THE DOOR AND FLINGS THE PRONE DAVE THROUGH.

THERE'S NO LIGHT, HOWEVER, AND DAVE JUST SKIDS THROUGH AND STOPS ON THE OTHER SIDE.

TOM FALLS TO HIS KNEES, PANTING FOR BREATH.

DAVE SLOWLY GETS TO HIS FEET.

DAVE   (CONT.) Fucking nutcase, that's what you are! It was always in her. You could see it! From the moment you met her! You could see it.

TOM   That's not true.

DAVE   It's LIFE, Tom. You can't make them want it. You've said so a thousand times. They've got to want it for themselves.

TOM   It wasn't in her.

DAVE   Whatever, you fuckcase.

TOM   When I met her. It wasn't in her.

PAUSE.

DAVE   You're telling me you…

TOM   She was content… when I met her. She was content.

DAVE   You poor fuck. (PAUSE) Well, that's one for

the books then. She told me to tell you something you know?

TOM LOOKS UP AT HIM.

DAVE   (CONT.) But then you threw me through the fucking door and I forgot it.

TOM   What now, then?

DAVE   What you mean, what now? What always now? We go on. Same as we always do. Same fucking people we always were. That's the whole point of it, ain't it? Come on, I'll buy you a fucking drink and you can talk me into not sacking your arse.

DAVE GOES TO EXIT BUT TOM MAKES HIS WAY TO THE TABLE AND PULLS OUT A FORM.

DAVE WATCHES HIM AS HE STARTS WRITING. HE PAUSES, SIGHS, AND THEN HEADS BACK TO THE TABLE.

DAVE   (CONT.) For fuck's sake. (HE SITS) You realize there's no coming back, right?

TOM   I do.

DAVE   And you realize there's no chance in you even finding her.

TOM   I don't.

DAVE   You won't even remember her.

TOM   You don't know that.

DAVE   Of course we fucking do. (PAUSE) You'll die, you know. Eventually. Everyone does!

TOM   Then I'll die.

DAVE   You've only known her a week!

TOM   David; we're not made for this. This perpetuity! This… repeat. The same things… We're not supposed to be like this, this endless counting out the days! We're not! I don't want to go through the same loops again and again and again. I don't want to do that anymore. So I'll die. That'll be one more door to walk through, won't it! One more question I don't have the answer to. But this! This… existing! I want to change. And if LIFE is change then LIFE it is.

DAVE   You been listening to your own fucking speeches again.

TOM   (PUTTING THE PEN DOWN) There. It's done.

DAVE LOOKS AT THE PAPER.

DAVE   Fuck you. I'm not talking you out of it.

TOM   I wouldn't want you to.

DAVE   Alright, fuck it, for the file. The company takes no liability for the extent of your life, nor does it promise promotion or satisfaction. What we offer you is change and the ability to use it. Whether you do so or not is completely up to you. Welcome to the company, you fucking moron.

TOM   No urge to come with me, then?

DAVE   Go fuck yourself.

THEY MAKE THEIR WAY OVER TO THE DOOR. AS THEY DO SO WE HEAR A RECORDING OF TOM'S EARLIER SPEECH.

TOM   (RECORDED) Because LIFE, ladies and

gentlemen, LIFE is something we choose. It does not come to us. It does not seek us out. We got to look for it.

Only thing you got to ask yourself is; is it gonna be the same door, the one you walked in through? Or is it gonna be a new one. A special one, the very epitome of a once in a lifetime's offer!

Everybody… At some point everybody has thought about walking through this door. There's a reason more people use us than any other supplier. Everyone has thought about walking through that door!

You're here tonight then you've thought about it. You're here tonight then you've read our literature, you've seen what LIFE has to offer! I'm not going to give you some great spiel about how great we are, or how great life is with us – how much better we are than our competitors!

No. It ain't about that! It's about you. What you want. What you want out of the experience.

A new start! A new LIFE!

All we need for a new life… is a new door.

AT THE DOOR THEY PAUSE, DAVE'S HAND ON THE HANDLE.

TOM   David, this is right. This is how we're supposed to feel. Trepidation. Uncertainty. This is what it means to be alive. Cocoon-less.

DAVE OPENS THE DOOR.

DAVE   Go fuck yourself.

AS HE DOES SO THE AUDIENCE ARE BLINDED BY A BRIGHT LIGHT.

SCENE 7
WHEN THE LIGHT FADES TOM AND JULIA ARE
STANDING AT OPPOSITE ENDS OF THE STAGE,
FACING THE AUDIENCE.

BOTH SPEAK, OVERLAPPING.

TOM   I was born in late September. I grew up on a council estate in Reading.

JULIA I was born early August. I grew up on a farm, outside Melbourne.

I spent my youth playing football which, I think, is the only real memory I had until the age of about 13. Fifteen a side, three games at once, kick it for the goal kind of thing.

I spent my youth at the beach or riding horses, though, more at the beach really. My parents were imigrants, from Iran and I don't think they really knew anything about farming or anything but I guess the idea appealed to them so there it was.

And it was a good childhood. Lots of getting in trouble and I wasn't exactly I think the easiest of children to deal with and there were three of us, so...

And it was a good youth. You know, lots of sunshine and people to hang out with. We had this dog, Lucy who kind of got usurped when my sister came along and we travelled. All of us.

We weren't well off so I never even thought about

My parents had family everywhere so we used to

travelling. We went to Brighton for holidays and I remember thinking donkeys were a really big thing and my father took me to see Reading play QPR and that was big deal for me.

spend a lot of time with them. London, Egypt, Canada.

And I learnt to surf. Naturally. Which is what all Australians do as soon as we can walk. And I took a gap year before university and went to India, which was a real eye opener for me.

I went to university in Essex. No one in my family had ever been to university so it was kind of a big deal and I studied the business which, actually, is not as bad as it seems.

I went to university in Melbourne. Dance. Which meant lots of sensitive boys and great, meaningful sex, but not much more than that. But it's a great city to do that in, lots of great nightlife and, I know it's silly but it really seemed like I was an artist, you know?

After that I kind of wandered for a while, this job and that. I did my Masters and took some odd jobs, nothing progressive.

I thought I was a painter, but really, that was this whole thing? I used to sell cards on street corners but I think people only bought them because they fancied me.

And then I met Abby.

And then I met Kyle.

She was working for this firm I was with. One of those cold calling companies and I was looking for a little cash and she was at reception and we hit it off, then and there and she… she was wonderful, you know. And… it wasn't even as if I was looking for something but there she was and there I was before I know it we were married.

Not even my kind of guy. Too handsome. Too down to earth. I'd been dating musicians and he was a carpenter and that was never really my thing? But we got married… Three months. Just like that!

We had Lincoln the next June and Hartley eighteen months later.

I remember we were… so happy!

I got a job in Singapore, working for one of the banks and went over there for a couple of years and I started my own consulting company, nothing grand, but it was mine, you know, ours! And Abby started to teach…

We spent five years in the back of a van driving around Australia and then, because the kids were getting a bit old and they needed a proper education, Kyle got this job in London and we all moved there.

She was the love of my life

He was the love of my life.

We never had kids. Wanted them, but never had them. We did think about adoption? But we were overseas a lot. France after Singapore and I guess it

We were together for, what thirty-eight years and if I'd been paying attention to the lights instead of fiddling with my phone it might have been thirty

wasn't really us, you know? We travelled a lot. America mostly. I loved the south, you know? All those open greens coming to a sudden stop next to desert, next to crops? Maybe a past life, who knows, perhaps I was Jefferson.

-eight more, you know what I mean? And… I don't think we stayed in one place longer than a couple of years and the kids… I mean, life is the best education, isn't it? And passing on that idea that you can live anywhere, do anything. That's the most important thing you can pass on to a person!

There was one other woman.

There was one other man.

I'd…

We bought a church. You know one of those do up-able things.

Abby was still in France and I was looking at apartments, in London.

And this man came to look at one of them.

And I don't know what it was…

And I don't know what it was…

It only lasted about a week.

It was nothing really, only…

It stayed with me.

Just…

Stayed with me.

I don't know why I brought it up.

I don't know why I brought it up.

LIGHTS DOWN.

END OF ACT 3.

Also by

Thomas Alexander

Thomas Alexander

THE VISITOR

BY

THOMAS ALEXANDER

THE VISITOR

WHEN THE LOVER OF A FAMOUS WRITER GOES MISSING IN A WAR RAVAGED COUNTRY HE BRIBES HIS WAY INTO A JAIL TO QUESTION HER HUSBAND, A MISSIONARY, WHO IS BEING TORTURED AS A TRAINING EXERCISE BY HIS CAPTORS.

ALONE IN THE CELL, THE TWO START A DIALOGUE ABOUT THE NATURE OF BELIEF.

BELIEF IN GOD, LOVE, AND POLITICS.

74

MURDER ME GENTLY

By

THOMAS ALEXANDER

"ONE MAN... ONE WOMAN... AND THE QUEST FOR JUSTICE IN AN UNJUST WORLD"

MODERN DAY RUSSIA THROUGH THE MEDIUM OF FILM NOIR

BLENDING REAL LIFE EVENTS WITH COMEDY AND INTRIGUE, **MURDER ME GENTLY'S** UNIQUE PERSPECTIVE ON THE WORLD OF RUSSIAN POLITICS AS SEEN THROUGH THE LENS OF FLIM NOIR, SPANS THE ASSASINATION OF INTERNATIONALLY RENOWNED JOURNALISTS, PUTIN'S REACH FOR THE RETURN OF SOVIET SATELITE STATES, AND THE INFLITRATION OF GOVERNMENT BY OLIGARCHS AND CRIMINALS.

PROVIDING A DAMMING INDICTMENT OF THE WEST'S INABILITY TO HALT MOSCOW'S POLICY OF EXPANSIONISM **MURDER ME GENTLY** LENDS A THEATRICAL EXPOSE TO THE VERY REAL WORLD OF CORRUPTION AND GREED IN INTERNATIONAL POLITICS TODAY.

A CONMAN, A DISGRACED INTERPOL AGENT, A MAFIA BOSS, A CIA SPOOK, AND THE SECRET TO THE FUTURE ALL UNITE IN AN UNLIKELY ALLIANCE IN A LOVE AFFAIR THAT WILL DEFINE THE FATE OF THE WORLD IN THOMAS ALEXANDER'S

... MURDER ME ... GENTLY!

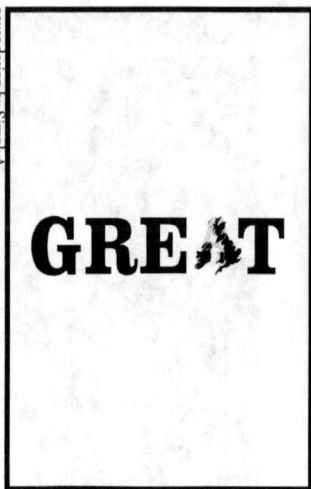

GREAT

GREAT

BY

THOMAS ALEXANDER

A REMOTE ROOM IN THE THROES OF
WINTER.

THE ONCE GREAT MAN LIVES ALONE
NOW WITH HIS SON,

AN OLD FRIEND HAS COME TO VISIT.
HE HAS CLIMBED UP FROM THE VIL-
LAGE IN ORDER TO OFFER THE OLD
MAN ONE LAST CHANCE TO ESCAPE
THE ENCROACHING WINTER THAT
IS ABOUT TO TAKE HIM, STIRRING
UP MEMORIES OF BETTER TIMES AND
THE WARMTH OF SUMMER.

BEGAT

BY

THOMAS ALEXANDER

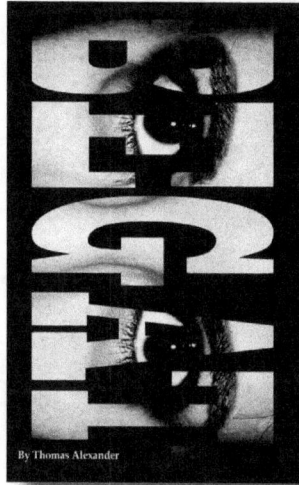

IN A COUNTRY, AFTER THE WAR, A JUDGE THROWS A DINNER PARTY, SEEKING SUPPORT AGAINST A POWERFUL MINISTER WHO HAS RAPED AND KILLED A SERVANT GIRL.

BUT THE JUDGE HIMSELF IS THE TARGET TONIGHT, AND THE SHADOW OF THE WAR HE SO DESPERATELY WANTS TO LEAVE BEHIND THREATENS TO ENGULF HIS FAMILY AS A YOUNG WOMAN SEEKS REVENGE FOR THE SINS OF HIS PAST.

HAPPINESS

BY

THOMAS ALEXANDER

ON A REMOTE HEADLAND IN NORTH
WALES A MAN AND HIS PARAPLEGIC
SON DREAM OF LIFE BEYOND THE
CONFINES OF THEIR FOUR WALLS.

BUT WHEN A WOMAN OFFERS THEM
THE ESCAPE THEY SO CRAVE THEY
FIND THEY ARE BOUND BY MORE
THEN THEIR DREAMS.

THE JEALOUSY OF A BORED POLICE-
MAN AND THE KINDNESS OF A MAIL
ORDER BRIDE SET THEM ON A PATH
OF HOPE AND DESTRUCTION.

THE LAST CHRISTMAS

cover design by SimplyA

THE LAST CHRISTMAS

BY

THOMAS ALEXANDER

IT'S NEWS!

WHEN AN EMBATTLED NEWSROOM RECEIVES A POTENTIALLY EARTH SHATTERING STORY MINUTES BEFORE AIR ON CHRISTMAS DAY THE CAREFUL EQUILIBRIUM OF THE TEAM IS SHATTERED AND OLD DIVIDING LINES COME TO THE FORE, TURNING CO-WORKER AGAINST CO-WORKER.

SET IN REAL TIME AND INCORPORATING ACTUAL AND INTERCHANGEABLE NEWS EVENTS THE LAST CHRISTMAS PITS SOCIAL POLITICS AGAINST JOURNALISTIC INTEGRITY IN A BATTLE OF THE ETHICS.

GOD

By

Thomas Alexander

When the named partner of a small law firm dies, leaving large debt, the remaining misfits of the firm are forced to take on just about any client available, including a litigious soccer-mum who would like to sue God for the death of her husband – hit by a lightning bolt on the 15th hole of a municipal golf course.

The Trial becomes complicated however, when an indigent with no background and a canny knack of knowing everyone's background enters the courtroom claiming to be 'God'.

Batting back and fore between the courtroom and the personal lives of the lawyers, 'God' is a fast paced courtroom drama/comedy that uses original staging and non-linear storytelling to provide a lighthearted, but complex social drama.

The Family

By

Thomas Alexander

Today, for the first time in longer than anyone can remember, the family are gathering. They are gathering to celebrate the engagement of the matriarchal niece, they are gathering to celebrate the last birthday of the patriarch, they are gathering to welcome home the prodigal son and his beautiful girlfriend and they are going to celebrate all this with a slideshow.

Candid photographs. Photographs of things no one thought anyone else knew about. Photograph taken when no one else was there.

It's all coming out today. In black and white for everyone to see. The remnants of child abuse, infidelity, loss, destruction and missed birthday parties. It's all coming out. It's going to be a long night. Possibly forever.

The Recruitment Officer

By

Thomas Alexander

Tom, a charming Yankee recruiter, comes to an unspecified English town and falls in love with the conference centre manager, Julia.

But what exactly is he recruiting for? Why does everyone who joins never come back and what is on the other side of the door

where do the recruits go after signing up?

An existential love story that asks questions of who we are, what we want from life and whether we're getting it, The Recruitment Officer is a remodelling of the 1706 play by George Farquhar. *The Recruiting Officer*

WRITER'S BLOCK

BY

THOMAS ALEXANDER

PAUL BLOCK WAS ONCE A PROLIFIC WRITER. A RECIPIENT OF BOTH THE PEN AND FAULKNERAWARDS AND THE AUTHOR OF OVER TEN DIFFERENT NOVELS, HE WAS ONCE CONSIDERED THE UK'S MOST UP AND COMING WRITER UNTIL, AT THE AGE OF FORTY, HE SUFFERED A NERVOUS BREAKDOWN.

TEN YEARS LATER THE WORLD HAS FORGOTTEN PAUL BLOCK. HOLED UP IN HIS STUDY HE HAS BEEN WORKING ON THE SAME FIRST PAGE OF HIS NEW NOVEL FOR NEARLY FIVE YEARS, KEPT COMPANY BY ONLY HIS MAID, A FOUL MOUTHED IRISH HIT-MAN, A VETERAN OF THE BATTLE OF GETTYSBURG AND A NINETEEN FORTIES FEMME FATALE.

TODAY, ALL THAT'S GOING TO CHANGE. PAUL HAS A BUSY DAY AHEAD OF HIM. FIRST HE'S GOING TO KILL A PERSISTENT AND CHARMLESS YOUNG REPORTER WHO WANTS TO DO A PIECE ON 'WRITER'S BLOCK' AND THEN HE'S GOING TO HAVE A RARE VISIT FROM HIS SON WHO'S BRINGING HIM BAD NEWS AND A NEW COUCH.

WITH A MISSING BODY AND A SON WHO HATES HIM, PAUL MUST FINALLY RID HIMSELF OF HIS PROTAGONISTS IF HE'S EVER GOING TO STAY OUT OF JAIL, AND FINISH THAT FIRST PAGE.

Japan, 1945 – A Family At War

When a wandering priest escaping a troubled past is taken in by a prominent family, a quiet city in northern Japan is forced to confront the dark shadows of war seeping into their lives in ways they could never have anticipated.

With its townsmen scattered throughout the farthest ends of a desperate empire in a final defence against the encroaching West, the idyllic northern city of Morioka, far removed from the harsh realities of the front, is largely left to itself.

THOMAS ALEXANDER

A Scattering of Orphans

But when a prominent doctor is conscripted and sent to Manila, his sister is left as head of the household and must deal with a young priest living at the bottom of their garden with a large collection of maps and strange knowledge of English.

As the cold hand of war approaches, each person must choose their own destiny and place in the new world.

ALEXANDER

Commemorating the 70th Anniversary of the end of WW2! A trilogy spanning the length of the war from the viewpoint of an ordinary Japanese family.

Thomas Alexander

The Disingenuous Martyr

omas Alexander

Beyond The Noonday Sun

Offering a unique perspective through the eyes of a rural Japanese family into the impact of history's bloodiest war to date, *A Scattering of Orphans* is one family's attempt to make sense of a changing world amidst the desolation of war, both home and abroad.

OF THE SUN

THOMAS ALEXANDER

The Recruitment Officer